My Waffle Dreams

norman rawlings

iUniverse, Inc.
Bloomington

My Waffle Dreams

iUniverse books may be ordered through booksellers or by contacting:

iUniverse
1663 Liberty Drive
Bloomington, IN 47403
www.iuniverse.com
1-800-Authors (1-800-288-4677)

Because of the dynamic nature of the Internet, any web addresses or links contained in this book may have changed since publication and may no longer be valid. The views expressed in this work are solely those of the author and do not necessarily reflect the views of the publisher, and the publisher hereby disclaims any responsibility for them.

Any people depicted in stock imagery provided by Thinkstock are models, and such images are being used for illustrative purposes only.

Certain stock imagery © Thinkstock.

ISBN: 978-1-4502-9909-1 (sc)
ISBN: 978-1-4502-9910-7 (ebook)

Printed in the United States of America

iUniverse rev. date: 03/03/2011

Dedicated to those that never gave up on me: Keno, Jet, Becks, Todd and Kelly, Shel, Jeffy and Em, Kate, and B&D.
But most of all...I offer this book up to Max and Morgan. They are my reasons and I'd still be lost without them.

Prologue

Sometimes I just giggle at what I hear my kids say. At the time of this writing, I'm witnessing a debate develop between my 10 year old son and his younger sister on the cerebral properties of Saturday morning cartoons. He feels as if they are moronic and lack a certain educational purpose. She thinks he is a "big pile of monkey poo." It's really astonishing to me the clarity and singular purpose that children have when they try to get their point across to one another. For instance, what better words could be spoken to complete or add a definitive statement to an argument than "…I'M TELLING MOM!" Who among us would not love to stand in front of a judge during traffic court and after being told to pay the entire amount of the fine calmly retort back, "You smell funny" and then run from the courtroom laughing hysterically. I'd give any amount of money to look back at some of my bosses I've had in my lifetime and exclaim at the highest volume I could muster "YOU'RE A JERK WEED DUFUS!" and have it actually mean something or change the nature of our relationship.

I have a very good friend that has a little brother about ten years our junior. As a boy, he was a very polite kid. A little goofy but who among us doesn't see the goofiness in all little brothers. He always seemed to be in the way and even if he wasn't he was a clear target for our ridicule. We were punks. He was present. What more is required for the comedy to ensue? And despite the overwhelming force he was up against he had a standard response to much – if not all – our bullying behavior. It was such an encompassing announcement that to this day I use it in my daily vernacular. He'd stand as fierce and as proud as a General on a battlefield and exclaim, "You're not the all-time boss of me." Passion and power mixed with poetry with purpose. No more crystal clear sentiments have ever been uttered in the history of debate. Socrates would have been proud.

For the better part of my life I've always put my words down on paper and somehow things seemed to make a little more sense afterwards. The experts might have you believe that this practice would be a calculated pause toward releasing any tangled thoughts getting in the way of your thoughts In short, writing helps your emotions catch up to your cognitive process. Fine, I'll buy that. However it is defined, what you are going to dive into as you read this book is simply my way of responding back to those circumstances that have wandered into my life and what I've ventured out and found on my own. Whether or not they find some similarities or connections with your daily existence will only be determined by your nodding of heads or a slight smile as you read them. I wish I could watch you all flip through the pages.

Of course, there is always the possibility you'll label this book as superlative babble and meaningless to your own journey. In response to this I say, "I know you are but what am I?"

Enjoy.

Norm Rawlings

Three Months

On Memorial Day in 1991, a young mother gives birth to a little girl. It's a bright and clear morning in Tacoma, Washington and as she looks outside her thoughts are not comforted by the brilliance of the dawning sun. She is not relieved over the ordeal of childbirth or breathless over the miracle of childbirth. Her thoughts were trapped inside the confines of two simple words: "Three Months". The young woman had just given birth to a child a full three months premature who dusted the scales at a feeble two pounds and was dangerously close to death.

The delivery was the undesired climax of three frantic weeks by the medical staff at Tacoma General Hospital to prevent the birth from taking place. Understandably, three months is nowhere near enough time for a child to become fully developed in her mother's womb. Any infant delivered during this precarious stage in a pregnancy is bound to be fraught by dangerous medical conditions. As it is with most premature babies, the inability for oxygenation on their own was first and foremost in the minds of the professionals at Tacoma General. However, her tiny, undeveloped lungs were only precursors facing the doctors. The child's low birth weight spawned many other health risks (collapsed lungs, hemorrhaging of the brain due to lack of oxygen, intestinal disease spawned from the death of undeveloped tissue, etc.) that – at any given hour – could mean the difference between life and death.

Each singular moment in the baby's life was either a stress relieving milestone (albeit it a brief one) or a heart wrenching setback that sent her mother reeling from stress and exhaustion. There was no "in between" episodes in those first few weeks. Every few hours were visited by medical emergencies that threatened the young child's life. Her frail, seemingly transparent body was warmed only by a light and a small plastic cloth. The tubes feeding her and keeping her alive long enough for her own strength to supersede that of technology gave her the appearance of a medical experiment rather than a human being.

And despite the cliffs of emotional fatigue she clung to, the young mother found within herself the ability to pray for strength outside of her own control. She discovered an unfamiliar faith through the release of her pain and uncertainty of what was to come. There was an inner submission to the understanding of what was secretly promised to her child. She felt a more comforting peace that was secured by nothing more than a love and connection to people she did not know but came to trust with the life of her daughter. She had no words for what was being done to her baby. She couldn't comprehend why all of it was happening to her. All she had was a daughter fighting for her life and the helpless realization that her struggle was no longer hers but that of her child's.

Hours became days. Days turned into weeks. The baby's color began to slowly improve. Droplets of precious oxygen within her own life giving blood started to replenish the areas of her body that desperately needed them the most. The tireless efforts of doctors and nurses began to pay lifesaving dividends. Her tiny seizures subsided. She began taking her own breaths. She was on her way.

On May 30th, 1991 at 7:13 a.m. in the Neonatal Intensive Care Unit of Tacoma General hospital a tiny child was born. She weighed a mere two pounds and was only 13.5 inches long. Her mother named her Arianna Chantelle. She bears a proud and miraculous name. Greek and French origins translated to "Holy One" and "Song". While it is true that the history of Memorial Day is based in large part on remembering those that have fought and died for our freedoms as American citizens, we would be remiss in not celebrating the bravery of the internal spirit of life that runs through all of us. It is the same spirit that motivates our men and women in the military and law enforcement to stand up and fight to protect those that can't stand up and protect themselves. It is a remembrance of the moral measurement and testimony of faith we have in each other and that of – at times – complete strangers. Yes, it is a day to commemorate that others fight and tragically die so we may have the finest that life has to offer. But even more than all of this, it is a day to remember the unflinching truth that we need each other in order to give life back to ourselves and to those that we love.

And if this miraculous child who came to know the world a full three months early (who is now celebrating 19 years in her mother's warm embrace) has taught us anything, it is the simple reminder of how good we all have it because of the sacrifice of others we don't know. For some of us, it is a memory steeped in faith that came one painful breath at a time. "…and a little child shall lead them."

A little child indeed. Happy Memorial Day.

Directions

Isn't it funny that the further down the road we get the more convinced that we're not going in the right direction? Even worse is that we are blissfully unaware of where the hell we are going in the first place. And ladies…before you pop off with one of your "it's just you guys not willing to ask for directions" spiel, let me just tell you that we don't have a problem asking which way to go. It's just that our desire to defile our manhood in such a besmirching manner depends wholly on the destination. For instance, if we are on our way to a wine and cheese tasting party sponsored by one of your co-workers in order to raise money for the gay, unborn, sea leopard pups then we'll never ask for directions in the fervent hope that we end up in Botswana infested with malaria and within inches of our own death. On the other hand, if we're on our way to some monumental event like our kid's wedding, the Superbowl, or wet t-shirt and jello shot night at Hef's then we'll ask for directions. Hell…we'll even spend a thousand dollars on state of the art GPS for our Ford Taurus *and* stop at every 7-11 and ask Abu for block by block instructions.

What I'm talking about is how we adapt to every different situation along the road and then interpret it as some grand scheme we thought we came up with on our own. Marriage comes to mind in this regard. I would highly doubt that any of us that have been down this idyllic – albeit pothole stricken - path have gone into it expecting that it will lead to being completely lost along the way. Unfortunately, that happens to 56 percent of us and sometimes more than once. Does that mean we are destined to fail on our journey, we didn't have the right instructions before we started, or that we suck at following these instructions in the first place? My answer is…regrettably…yes. We're going to fail at times along the way. Many of us don't have the game plan all figured out before we take the leap. Even more shockingly to some even if we had the right plan we somehow find a way to botch up the entire operation before "till death do us part." And while I'm a part of that 56th percentile, I would advise anyone to journey down the path again and expect failure. This time, however, you'll know where those potholes are located. You'll see that the language of their mind and the actions of their heart don't always mesh and sometimes…that's ok. You'll be able to find out if the dance outside of your cave is real or they're just trying to get you out into the open so they don't feel so alone.

And finally, you'll be able to understand that any notion you may have of your own "failure" has to be replaced with a sense of accomplishment in what you've learned. You haven't failed, folks. You haven't gotten lost. You found a new set of directions that will take you on a new journey. How bad can that be?

When you get there…ask for me. Hef and I will be six jello shots ahead of you.

Pale Blue Dot

I saw this documentary once on interplanetary violence and space discovery. Just the words "interplanetary violence" probably lost half of my reading audience and the other half whispers, "Oh God. Norm and his drivel again." Bear with me, as it's a pretty cool set of terms mentioned in conjunction with Carl Sagan in his book "Pale Blue Dot: A Vision of the Human Future in Space". Sagan was referencing the "Pale Blue Dot" photograph, a title he gave to a picture taken by the spacecraft Voyager 1 in 1990 as it was leaving our solar system. Voyager 1 was launched in 1977 and 13 years later had reached the edge of the solar system as we know it. It had – up till this point – been pointing its cameras outward into the vast expanse of the universe to look for.... whatever; new planets, new stars, new worlds, new hopes, new places to put a Starbucks, etc. Sagan himself asked NASA that at the point where Voyager 1 was leaving the solar system that the lens be turned around to take a picture of Earth against the boundless backdrop of space. Hence, from 3.7 billion miles away, we see the world we live in as a pale blue dot against a canvas of dark nothingness.

Wow. That's friggin' depressing when it's put that way. Thanks, Carl, you morbid bastard.

I've seen the Pale Blue Dot photograph. Type it into any search engine and you'll see it too. It's one of those kinds of photos / pictures that remind me of my daughter's old "Where's Waldo?" books. You know it's there somewhere. Your face is pressed against the screen or the page and you're going blind trying to discover it. I did the same thing with the Voyager photograph, but damned if it just looks like a black TV screen in a dark room. But then, just when you're about to give up, there it is. And if you're like me you swear under your breath and are overcome by this awesome sense of insignificance as it is juxtaposed against the colossal and infinite field of our existence. Perhaps Sagan was right (and who am I to say he wasn't) when he wrote "When you make the finding yourself...even if you are the last person on the Earth to see the light...you'll never forget it."

I like to write down my thoughts and experiences. Sometimes these writings morph into something that I can put on display to see if anyone else feels the same way I do about life's little peccadilloes. But for the most part, my inner struggles have been just that...internal; very personal and extremely private. These past few months have been a struggle for me. I've been looking for answers and trying to find the reasons behind why the curveballs been coming at me like bullets from a gun. As I'm doing this, I've been trying to remain healthy enough to get up out of the dirt and do it all over again the next day. If the overall disturbance of my own interplanetary violence in the past six months has taught me anything it's that the more you think you're capable of discovering the light on your own the more the universe (and to me, its Creator) teach you that you are not really supposed to.

With all due respect to Mr. Sagan, I'll never see the truth that way. I'll never find the pale blue dot of my life and my role in it by staring at the damn photograph without asking for help. And – at the risk of sounding preachy – I would doubt any of you will either. I've been blessed by an amazing group of friends and family. I've been even further honored by re-discovering some people again after so many years that – in my adolescent and therefore ignorant life – thought I knew but only now discovered how amazingly warm, compassionate, and unique they truly are. I've even been re-introduced to family of friends that have extended warmth and sincerity to me just because they are that way and they knew me "way back when." I've been loved individually and indiscriminately by them as I stand amongst their presence completely contaminated by the pitfalls of the past six months. They didn't give a rip about my state of being in which they discovered or rediscovered me. They only care about the truth and the light and that I couldn't see either of them from where I was standing.

Now I can. And just like in the "Where's Waldo" pictures, I'll never **not** know where to find that goofy face with that goofy grin. I'll always be able to recognize that however far the eye travels from the image, I'll know that there – in the vastness of space – I can and will find love.

Crazy Little Thing Called....

I've been thinking about women lately. Well, let me clarify that I generally think about women in some fashion or another; emotionally, physically, spiritually, parentally, etc. etc. I am father to one. I was married to one. I've been in love with one. The most powerful expression a man can experience and appreciate is the love and support of a woman. There is nothing else in this life that is more fulfilling and more rewarding.

Disclaimer aside, I'm convinced that the majority of them are crazier than shithouse rats. They are the most mysterious and outrageous creatures ever to grow wild in the jungle. Who else can provide such life giving love and, in the matter of moments, take it away? Who else can take you to the deepest caverns of your own soul and teach you things so completely foreign about yourself and at the same time be totally oblivious to the havoc they can trigger in your mind and in your heart? Who else can act like an angel one minute and a dragon the next and completely pass off this metamorphosis as breezily as a bird changing direction in flight? Who else but an insane person can only order a salad as their main course but then eat half of your garlic cheesy fries and down three Coronas? And finally only some sort of biological freak could wake up 6am, go jogging, head to the gym for yet another workout, put in 10 hours of hard core housekeeping, chauffeuring, cooking, selling, teaching, and wine tasting and then fall asleep in her spot whispering that she doesn't have enough time in her day to…to…zzzzzzz.

Let me set the record straight: I'm not bitter towards women. I'm not angry about some version of "love lost" or "love unrealized" or "love unexpected" or "love or something like it." I sincerely want what everyone else wants, however I will not settle when it comes to matters of my own heart. I don't think any of you should either.

So despite the hilarity of their actions, despite the desperately maniacal nature in which they themselves try to find love at any cost and regardless of the wake they sometimes leave in their quest to do so, I'm forever grateful that they, too, want the same thing.

The hook to all of this madness is to be laughing when we find each other and not cry so much when we don't.

One Foggy Day

Humans have a ridiculous way of complicating the hell out of things. We take the most mundane elements and making them mysterious and complex. I'm no exception. I'm guilty of turning the simplest stuff and confusing the shit out of it. Let's take fog, for instance. It has been implemented in movies, books, or scary campfire yarns as this shadowy veil of evil that masks the pending destruction of every stupid teenager who decides to venture away from the strength of the group.

"What was that sound?" says idiot polo shirt yuppie boy named Dexter.

"It is a boat buoy banging against the dock, genius." replies sensible, hippy dressed hot chick named Raven that always seems to survive despite the fact that we get no frontal nudity out of her for the whole picture (damn PG-13 rating).

"No it wasn't." whispers Dexter. "There was a sound that came out of the fog. It came from past the blood soaked chain saw and that mutilated body of Carl by the boat house. It's hard to see it because of the fog. Did I mention there was fog? It sure is foggy out."

THE FOG! Ooooooh…..

John Carpenter had us frozen in 1980 with his movie, "The Fog." There is a legendary scary haunted house and overall macabre attraction facility in Maryland call "Legend of the Fog" and when I went online to Google "scary, deathly, spooky fog" I got 1.3 million results. However, when I Googled "funny, happy, goofy fog" I got a tenth of the results. I guess the internet has a morbid fascination with fog and either wants to see the hippy hot chick naked (who doesn't, let's be honest), Sure-to-die Dexter get diced up all over the dock, or Carpenter make a sequel called "The Fog: This Time It's Personal".

But before we start making funeral arrangements for our friends who have gone off to check on the spooky sounds, let's cut to the chase of what fog really is. I looked it up. The National Oceanic and Atmospheric Administration has a much more scientific description of fog: "Fog is when a cloud touches the ground."

Huh? THAT'S IT?! "...when clouds touch the ground?" Surely it must be something more magical than that. They must have a reference to the juxtaposition of heavenly and earthly bodies engaging in an epic struggle for control of the middle earth. It must be about the lust for that mystical convergence of the four elements of the universe; earth, air, fire, and water. It has to spark a catalyst of events that make the known unknown, the visible invisible. And by doing so it evaporates all rational thought between Full Frontal Nudity with the Back Tattoo and Dexter the Sure-to-Die Wonder Dork.

Nope. "When a cloud touches the ground" is all we are left with. Oh sure, if you want to get all uppity on me we can get into the colossally mind numbing details of the density of the cloud and its relation to mist. I can drop you into a coma with meteorological details on how these two bodies pass each other in the air and how volatile solar radiation and the normal temperature of the earth's crust converge on these dense particles of water hovering above the ground. But who has time for that crap? Dexter sure as hell doesn't. Heavy air and water descending out of the sky to touch the ground. That's it. That's fog.

It's shortly before 5 am and I'm looking out over Hood Canal in western Washington. There was a pretty wicked rainstorm the night before. Those who live in this area and call it home are sure to recognize these types of mornings. It's grey and green. The air is calm and soaked from another spring storm. Fog has settled over the still glassy water of the hundreds of inlets and coves of this canal. Patches of it linger amongst the trees on the steep hills rising above the water. Amongst the evergreens, fog seemingly hides from the warmth of the dawning sun, desperate to hold onto its association with something real before its ascent back to the heavens.

I told you I'd complicate things. If I had a way to shut off this line of thinking in my brain believe me...I'd be first in line to buy that wonder potion. But when I look out over the water and I see the fog blanketing that which I knew to be there the day before it reminds me that it's only a precursor to that which I have to face again today. It will be the same way tomorrow. And the next day...and the next. To me, when I see the secrecy of those heavenly clouds obscuring my vision for just a few hours, I can't help but wonder if this is one of God's little gifts; not giving me all I ask for all at once. Watching the fog lift and disappear in pieces to reveal the world I must face again is like an artist slowly sliding a shroud from a masterpiece so as to create the sense of excitement of what lay underneath. And it all happens one water particle at a time.

The brilliant C.S. Lewis wrote "I believe in Christianity as I believe that the sun has risen: not only because I see it, but because by it I see everything else." In this ever amplified world of energy drinks, carpe diem bumper sticker wisdom, and high octane mental stimulation through electronic means try to resist the urge to go screaming down the path like Dexter. More often than not life, death, and Raven the hot chick will present themselves to you if you simply take the time to recognize the moments when the heavens touch the earth. I guarantee that if you take a moment's pause then the "everything else" after the fog lifts will seem far less complicated.

Five Minutes

It's really amazing what can transpire in someone's life in such a short period of time. We've all heard the comparisons regarding time and how one minute for a football coach and that same minute for a surgeon can spell out the difference between victory and death. Or perhaps one year for a child and one year for a convict serving a life sentence may mean very little to each other. My point is that time is relative and needs very little coaxing on our part in order to develop or unfold the fabric of our destinies, if you believe in that sort of thing. Which…unfortunately… I do.

We pick up the story of a young man living a relatively decent life. He has a young wife, a young son, and a small house with a large mortgage. He is in a job which is less than personally fulfilling but the paychecks come regularly and the work is not as stressful as it could be. He has a good heart, a sharp mind, and isn't afraid to make new contacts, new friends, and can work a room accordingly. His son is happy. His wife is happy with both her "boys" and there is even a cat that doesn't crap where it isn't supposed to and loves raw hotdogs and eats popcorn. It's a fine little existence for a fine young man.

One stormy night, long past midnight but well before the dawn, our young hero awakes to a loud dull thud coming from downstairs. He is jolted out of bed, short of breath, and looks around the room to get his bearings. His wife is sleeping soundly which is alarming considering she is such a light sleeper. Surely she would have heard what he heard. He sat like a stone only hearing his own breath in the eerily silent room and listened for any other noise coming from downstairs. He hears knocking about and footsteps and muffled voices and quickly determines that there are burglars in his house. He reaches for his cell phone on the nightstand and quickly dials 911. Whispering to the operator his location and the situation, she instructs him to secure his family in a locked room and do not go downstairs. The police are on the way. He slips out of bed quietly and breathlessly tiptoes to his son's room and lifts him from his crib and carries him back to his still sleeping wife. Laying him beside her, she stirs and looks up at him sleepily and whispers, "Was he crying?

"No. There are people in the house. I called the cops. Stay here and lock the door behind me."

Not one to handle a crisis of this nature well, she gasps and grabs her young son and follows her husband to the door and turns the latch behind him as he slides out of the room. He still hears the voices despite the fact that his heart is pounding through his chest and up into his throat. At the top of the stairs, the floor creaks slightly underneath him and the whispers below stop suddenly. He freezes, half expecting he will hear hurried footsteps toward the door and half hoping they will continue talking so they will remain and then the police will catch them in the act. He hears nothing but the wind pushing the rain against the windows.

He makes the first move. He creeps down the stairs, fists clinched and ears alert for the slightest sound. He hears nothing. Reaching the bottom, he turns around the blind wall and peers down the long hallway to the living room. He sees two massive figures covered in shadows standing at the end of the hallway staring back at him. Both well over six feet tall and by the looks at their shapes easily in excess of 200 pounds. But their imposing silhouettes were not the most intimidating features. He could see their eyes. They were so intensely white that they pierced through the shadows and blackness of the house. They made no move toward him. They made no gesture toward each other. They didn't appear frightened or startled over being discovered. They continued to stare back at him coldly.

His voice cracked from fear. "You…..guys get the hell out of here. I've called the police. They are probably outside already." He didn't believe it either so he could only imagine what these monsters were thinking.

Without moving his head, his eyes shifted to the corner of the hallway where his wife kept an umbrella stand. They bought it one weekend and while the family was born and raised in the Pacific Northwest and never disgraced their heritage by actually using an umbrella, the wife liked its brass appearance and often put the odd golf club, broom, or yard tool in there to keep the hallway uncluttered. When his hand clasped around the shaft of a mini broom, his eyes went back toward the end of the hall and the figures were gone. He froze. He held his breath now fully hoping they rushed out of the house. No longer did he want justice. He just wanted them gone.

Hugging the wall on his slow creep down the hallway, gripping the broom as if it were the last branch before a deathly fall, he made his way to the living room. Stopping short of the entryway, he peered toward the front door and saw it securely locked and not open wide as he had prayed it would be. His memory screamed toward the backdoor and whether they escaped in that direction. As he stepped into the opened space of the living room, he heard a sudden whisper so close to his ear he felt the breath of it on his neck.

Then… a white flash of light. And then…nothing.

The police finally came. Not seeing any forced entry in the front door, they parted forces while one officer looked for a separate entrance. He found the backdoor unbolted and open, banging against the fence from the now increasing force of the wind. The senior officer, announcing his presence loudly into a still house, stepped into the darkness and shone his light to illuminate his path. His seasoned senses picked up a faint odor. His investigative instinct told him that what was going to happen had already happened. He was on high alert...even though he knew he was probably too late.

Five minutes. The amount of time it takes to reheat leftovers or greet old friends. A caring and efficient mother giving a newborn a bath in a new plastic tub was mere ticks of the clock. Weeding the small flower bed where he planted peppers to make his own salsa would fit in that window of time. And in the vast expanse of human history from the murder of Cain to the annihilation of a loving existence between father and son, five minutes is a mere blink of an eye.

There is no moral to this tragedy. This one doesn't have a happy ending no matter how many times I've looked for one. Life is crippled with these moments of loss but they are equally fulfilled with moments of time where we find ourselves in awe by each second of the day and its ability to usher in joy, peace and love. This is a true story as it stands today. Tomorrow it will be a memory for all of those that didn't know the young man, his young wife, or their young son. But in the five minutes you took out of your day to read this, five minutes were spent with them and by doing so turning the attention back to your own ticks of the clock.

Stop counting them. Make them count.

The Sighting

I recognized her the second I saw her back, even though it wasn't her. It all depends on the day, really. Sometimes, I would go weeks without thinking about her. Other times, it could be a month or two. This is just a lie, actually, because usually it's only a few hours but when I tell myself that I somehow feel better inside. Or maybe just a bit more drunk.

Laying awake so early plotting out my life seems like a fine waste of a Sunday, so I pull myself out of bed and dig through the remnants of clothes suitable for rain jogging and slip out into the still dark morning. I've never been much of a person interested in wasting valuable exercise time with mundane stretching, so veering a quick left and picking up my pace find myself at a nice clip down the path toward the park. Naturally, the second my breathing settles into a comfortable rhythm so does my thinking. In the short span of 14 minutes I manage to recall 22 years of damaging testimony to the inequities of my existence. I'm a world class rationalizer, so all events are tidied nicely into "how I take all that and fit it into all this" but for the most part I feel somewhat lifeless about the success of my past.

That's why thoughts of her are so disconcerting to me.

Moments with her seem to eradicate for me all the senselessness of those decisions. Without coming right out and saying it, thinking back on it all now just goes further in proving to me that some Higher Power had a hand in it all. Why on earth would He / She / It / Them put this person in my life and then take her away? Either a cruel joke or some cryptic lesson for me to figure out whilst I slowly going insane. How can she make me feel that every decision I've made, every instinct I followed, every consequence that ensued was designed specifically to direct me to that afternoon on that Tuesday by that body of water in that particular city. In one fell swoop, she managed to validate all that I had done and all that I wanted to do and wrap them up nicely in that breathtaking package.

A slow gradual turn to the left takes me up a minor hill which I lean into and pick up my pace a bit. While I've only gone a mile or less, I feel like it's been three and gaspingly curse myself for not getting out more to do this ridiculous ritual. Slight drops of rain on my now flush face tell me that I'm about three minutes from getting stuck in another Pacific NW rain / hail / snow / sunshine anomaly, so without thought make a hard right down a path I've never been down before but is sure to take me back to the direction of home simply based on the gut feeling that it veered in the direction from where I've been.

And that's when it happened.

It suddenly came to me in a hot flash of both clarity and crippling pain. While the ankles have never been the most trustworthy of joints in my body, they've never completely given out on me without so much as a twinge of a warning and never both of them at the same time. Crumpling to the ground and about ten seconds from crying in pain for the first time in 30 years, I look up and see her standing on the path in front of me. It had to be the shadows of dawn along with the sweat and raindrops in my eyes that caused this crazed vision, but still I couldn't stop staring in that direction and calling out to her in a whisper.

"Is that you?"

My voice barely broke the plane of silence of the dark. A slight ripple in the stillness but loud enough for her to hear to me, however far away she was. Coming back to reality was only possible because of the stabbing pain from my ankles and looking down half expected to see my legs blown off from the knee down. No protruding bones, no gross swelling, nothing but ugly shoes and mismatched socks. I was afraid to look back up for fear she was gone. Of course, when I did she was no longer there. After catching my breath, I pulled myself up to my feet and slowly the pain subsided. In fact, after a few more moments it was as if nothing had happened. Turning slowly, I walked back in the direction of home and began to chalk it up to yet another "sighting" and my aging and wearied mind.

The energy of one's soul is so powerful that it can collapse reality in such a way to make someone think...BELIEVE...that what they are going through is the most singular emotion in the world. Sometimes I think that if there could be one intangible thing that I could wish for and have it realistically take place in my life, it would be for the knowledge and validation of what I am feeling in my heart is shared by someone else.

The trick, I suppose, is finding that complex balance between wanting that information and not caring about it. But at the end of the day, all I can do is be thankful for those moments by the water.

The Young G.I.

Indulge me in a quick story, if you will. Nearly 50 years ago, a young G.I. walks into a bar in Southern California and sits down and orders a drink. He's had a relatively long day, tacked onto a long week which was – up to this point – an extension of a miserably long life and by god he's going to tie one on and cut loose. As many old songs go, however, his plans were interrupted by this cute young thing at the end of the bar. He buys her a drink, she returns the favor. A few hours pass by. Late afternoon turns into early morning and both young would be lovers clumsily fumble words and themselves into the street to hail cabs to go home.

Three weeks later they were married in Las Vegas.

Twelve months after that, the G.I. is overseas when his son is born. His wife had temporarily moved to the Pacific Northwest to be closer to family and for assistance during the last month of her pregnancy. The young G.I. is as pleased with life as he has ever been. He never knew that happiness and peace could come in his lifetime. His own existence had been riddled with foster home after foster home and then finally being raised by some distant "family" twice removed. There were "uncle-in-laws" and pseudo grandparents that never stood up to adopt him before so the streets of Toledo were his measuring stick on what men were supposed to do, how they were supposed to behave, and when they were supposed to fight. To the young G.I., however, those days were quickly disappearing in his rear view mirror. He was still in the service, home safely after his obligatory vacation to Southeast Asia, working on his pension and perfecting his craft as a mechanic. He had a young bride, a namesake son, and finally a clear and happy future.

Five years later, the young GI is honorably discharged from the service after fifteen years due to a hearing condition. After two failed attempts to add to his family (the second miscarriage coming seven months into the pregnancy) the young GI is beginning to wonder if life were simply too good to be true. The G.I.'s wife, a young nurse, never gives up hope and introduces the thought of adoption to her husband. He is understandably reticent. It never worked for him as a boy. Why should it work for him as an adult?

One day, his wife calls him and says – with her typical collectiveness – "How would you like an early Christmas, birthday, and father's day present?" He immediately recognizes what she is suggesting and hurries to the hospital where she is employed to find that a young boy, not 24 hours old, is on the trading block. The G.I.'s wife initially wanted a little girl and one was available, but she had a very serious heart condition and would require immediate medical attention that would cost a small fortune. The G.I. and his young wife debated amongst themselves for a few days this painful decision. In the end, they saw the obvious and practical choice of adopting the obscenely cute little boy with the one bad floppy ear and chocolate brown eyes.

Two years later, their idea of adopting due to medical conditions backfired on them when the G.I.s wife gave birth to a little girl. The couple chuckled at this lucky event and since the warranty had run out on their 2nd son they decided to keep him after all.

And on every anniversary – this September makes 49 and counting – and with every Mother's and Father's Day, this lucky draft pick sends a card to the G.I. and his young bride stating a simple yet completely encompassing emotion.

The card reads simply, "Thanks for picking me." Happy Anniversary, Bob and Donna. I'm happy to be on the team.

The Train

In the kneeling position, his son's head fit perfectly on his shoulder as he was facing him wrapped in a tattered Seattle Mariners fleece blanket. It is all he had to keep his little body warm while they waited for the early morning train. The man's hooded sweatshirt pulled low over his eyes so as to hide the effects of another long night. He wondered again how he was going to feed him when he got home. The boy never complained about the folded over butter sandwiches. He didn't make any mention of the brown, worm-holed crab apples picked off the ground from the neighbor's yard and put in his wrinkled brown paper sack. He never once whimpered how uncomfortable the old jeans were and how they've gotten to be a size too small. And while his dad knew that he needed his hair cut by someone with access to something sharper than kindergarten scissors, ten dollars went a lot farther on food then fashion.

They were all alone as they huddled together to keep warm in the damp and crisp break of morning. The waft of the hard-boiled egg on his son's breath revealed that he had forgotten to brush his teeth again. He made a mental note to go to the dollar store next to the job site and get some toothpaste.

As they waited for the train, the effort of constructing yet another smile and warm greeting for this now common "adventure" made him nearly want to vomit. He simply could not muster the feigned excitement on what was another morning without her; 192 days and counting.

She always kept the rhythm of the house. She always had the path planned out for both of "her boys." He felt comforted in the warm embrace of knowledge that he had finally broken free of the violence that raped his soul since he was a child. He discovered someone strong enough to peel away his old life to reveal one acceptable to others. Just when he was learning to live in this new skin, she was gone.

Haunting whispers of her and his past floated above his head like moths around a street lamp. The dirty yellow stove light and the hacking coughs of a dying refrigerator were his only company in their cramped, rented room. 4:00 a.m. was too early for a little boy to start his day, but there was no other choice. Without grumbling, without stalling, and even posting a half-baked attempt at a smile his little man pulled himself out of the *Toy Story* sleeping bag on the couch and into the bathroom for his morning ritual of target practice into the broken, clogged toilet. As he watched his son shuffle across the small room and he started to reel in his emotions in order to face another day. He was still caked in the sticky, sweat stained clothes he fell asleep in on the broken recliner. He just couldn't repeat her routine. He just didn't want to.

As the blackness of the horizon made way for the singular beacon of the train, he held him a little tighter and whispered, "Here she comes, buddy."

"Can I have the window seat this time, Dad?" he muttered under his breath as he was rubbing the sleep from his eyes.

"Sure, pal. Want to watch the sun come up?"

"No. Just want to count the poles."

Yes, Jack

The opportunity hit me rather quickly. I didn't understand it at first and then when I did I thought it was something that couldn't be explained. Six numbers in a row, the ones I always thought of, and then the dullness of fantasy set in. I didn't know I would feel this sick. Winning a fortune wasn't supposed to feel like a hangover.

They all came in small bunches. Two first...the obvious two. They came separate from one another which I thought was strange since they never travelled apart. The even more strange part was that he came first. He walked in and wanted "to talk." He's never wanted to talk. He's never walked in. Hell....he's never showed up.

Thirty minutes later she showed up. They were so damn terrible at coordinating their timing that it was painfully obvious that something was wrong. I asked him, then I asked her, then I wondered if I should be wary of some family conspiracy. When my brother and sister showed up I was convicted. I was the center of the worst planned intervention in the history of interventions. I couldn't hide my obvious smirk. If they only knew what I was about to tell them.

"Jack...we love you very much. We only want the best for you. But the emotional decisions you're making because of a woman we all think is destructive is tearing this family apart. She has cost you your life, your job, and your health. We only want you to be happy."

Oh...I'm happy, all right. How else would you feel if you just scored two hundred million dollars on six lottery numbers. As I was thinking of how to collect my fortune without paying a shitload to Uncle Sam, they were telling me how to make my life better by dumping the one person that saw the harmony and perfection in the way I was doing things. It's ironic when you think about it. Family was paddling toward me to get me to move away from my truth and she was treading water right smack in the middle of it and only asking for my time.

"So, you want me to do what exactly?" I was really enjoying this. This was turning into a litmus test for me to determine who was going to get some cash from me and who was going to sit in their living room afterwards wondering what the hell happened.

"We all think it's best if you end this relationship and get a normal job and get your life back on track." Of all the people, they chose the oldest sibling to do the talking. Nevermind that she was the last person in the world to be giving advice or to be pointing out the fundamental flaws in someone's life. The comedic drama of the intervention was briefly interrupted by my disdain for her. She being the one that came to me five years earlier for a loan to get back on her feet because all of her cheating was costing the marriage thousands per month in plane fares, hotel rooms, and Grand Cru Champagne. Another word out of her and the only things she gets from me is a package sent to her husband, her boss, and our mother of the surprisingly detailed photographs I have tucked away on my computer.

"Yes, Jack. And we just want the best for you." This coming from the man that used to beat me with jumper cables. Well...I've got something special for you too, old man.

"Let me see if I get this straight. You guys want me to dump her, move back home, get a real job, and live a life of quiet desperation?" This was all fun for a few minutes, but the contempt of it all started to sicken me. Besides, there was 212 million dollars and a month of drinks on a secluded beach in Tahiti with my name on it. I had plans to make, people to see and lives to enrich. Starting with my own and that of my children, who didn't give a rat's ass if I had one love in my life or a hundred because they knew that they were always above them all.

As I glanced around at their caring, somber faces my eyes dropped onto the youngest sibling. He was looking as if he wanted to be anywhere but where he was obviously dragged to. He returned my stare for a while and then we smiled at each other.

"What about you, Pauly? You in cohorts with the fam on this little breakdown?"

"Actually, Jack...I'm just here for a cold one. Got any in the fridge?"

That was it. Conversation was over. I just found my new beneficiary. I always liked him anyway. I made a mental note to rent a second beach house.

Bedroom, God, and the Campfire

Those of you with young children (or any children, for that matter) would, no doubt, recognize this scenario: It's 3:00am, you are sound asleep dreaming of sleeping. You are on clouds that are sleeping while there are other sleeping little angels all sleeping around them. The only element of your sleep that doesn't resemble a coma is the subconscious knowledge and harmony that your children are also fast asleep dreaming of race cars, ponies, baseball or licorice. And...just when you roll over for round two of deep REM sleep you open your eyes for a split second only to discover your young child is standing 12 inches from your face with her stuffed puppy and her pillow waiting for the invitation to crawl into bed with you. After you reach back into your throat to pull your heart out you either talk her back into her room or surrender the small portion of your bed she'll need to fall back asleep. The small portion, of course, turns into 80% of the total surface space of the mattress after she's done, but that's beside the point.

Sound familiar? You or your spouse are the haven of safety for your children in the middle of the night when the blowing wind, a distant siren, or the boogeyman happens to wake them up. It's one of those beautiful unwritten rules in that unpublished parental handbook that all of us seem to misplace on the way home from the hospital.

I have my children every other weekend. Even when I don't have them, I wake up at night sometimes and walk down the hall to their rooms at 3am only to discover that they are not there. When they are with me it's practically a sure fire guarantee that I will roll over, see them standing there in the shadows not wanting to wake me up, and surrender my sleep for either (or both) of them. I don't mind it so much. The every other weekend thing prompts me to soften my perspective on the boundaries of whose bed belongs to who. Plus, their breathing typically puts me into more of a deeper slumber than I've felt in many, many years.

So you can imagine my shock when - during a night when they were with their mother - that I rolled over and discovered not my 10 year old son nor my 8 year old little girl standing in the dark waiting for me to accept them but someone that I hadn't ever expected to see.

I opened my eyes and there, holding a cup of tea and staring intently at me, was God.

And you know something? He didn't look anything like I thought He would. He was shorter and looked like he wore the map of the world on his face and his hair was all askew. He was slightly hunched over as if trying to find a comfortable postion to stand. On hindsight, He struck me as resembling the offspring of Albert Einstein, Mel Brooks, and my mother. I crammed my fists into my eye sockets to blast the sleep from my vision. This, of course, is the universal way to clear your vision but the more I did it the less visible he became. It was as if I was looking through a waterfall at a statue but couldn't ever become focused on the details of the image. He spoke first.

"I never expected you to get to this point." He didn't sound frustrated or ashamed or disappointed in any way. It was more of a question than anything else.

"What point are you talking about?" The question surprised me a bit as I couldn't believe that that was what I was saying to God standing in my bedroom at three in the morning.

"You've ventured a little out a little past the shore, you've gone too deep into the forest. You're away from the campfire. You like metaphors, son. Pick one."

Still laying on my side and still squinting a bit to draw Him into vision more clearly, I started to see His point. There hasn't been a day or two that has passed in nearly 10 years that I haven't felt isolated from the peace that we are all supposed to feel in life. The old adage that "life isn't fair" can become a dangerous one if you take it too literally. It should be like a classroom or a playing field or a living room where you know that you can and are almost expected to make mistakes but there is a centerpoint you can retreat to when you get too far from good. I've always had the theory that the people on the overpass with cardboard signs and those that are safely in their cars are only separated by the ignorance of that centerpoint. They got too far from the campfire, lost their bearings, and either couldn't find their way back or didn't have anyone to lead them.

I was raised in a fairly decent home. I was given food and love and attention and for the most part a strong sense of what was right and wrong. If I didn't pick it up in my living room, I got it from my friend's parents or their family. Even with a solid background with a good family, there are so many of us that get lost in the currents of adult existence without so much as a compass to lead them toward what they feel is necessary to substantiate life, love, and happiness. Marriage won't do it. Children come pretty damn close to doing it. And even someone's religion can fall a bit short, although my Christian brethren would argue with me on this point. Your lives are amazing passages of time, folks. We create and define and choose the elements that animate it. We either trust which direction we are supposed to go based on some societal preconception of success and happiness or we blaze our own trail to try to reinvent the wheel. Yet...the volatility of a soulful expedition can quite easily abandon any and all foundation you have thought you had in the first place. In short, be advised....you go with your gut and it only takes a few wrong moves to end up on the overpass.

I've been blessed with good friends and a great family. The stranger in my bedroom would suggest that my children were a gift as well and one that I probably didn't deserve. However they ended up in my life...I am not me without them. Recently, there have been some paths that have led me away from my own centerpoint and I got to where the friendly voices around the campfire became more and more distant. It was only due to the help of a few dear people that I found my way back. I ask all of you to be on the lookout for those in your own life that are no longer celebrating with you or walking close to where you can see their faces without squinting through the fog. Stay close to them so that when they call out from the darkness, you can venture out to pull them back in.

You will sleep better at night...even if they are hogging all the bed.

Outer Limits

For the sake of protecting her identity, I'm going to call her "Mary". It's a nice name. She is a nice woman. And by "nice," I mean perfect. She is intelligent, funny, adorable, engaging, and so damn electric in a room that she makes other people wonder why they don't have more of a personality. When you can wonder that about yourself, then you know you've got a painfully attractive woman in the room.

I knew her when I first saw her. It was striking to see her stride across the floor toward me and even though I knew she was coming to me I felt in my heart I would never reach her. She just seemed too damn good. Most men feel that way about women. They don't' like to admit it but when they see someone like her they instantly feel their own faults and weaknesses and indiscretions and they just want to walk into the corner of the room and drink beer or else walk up to them and make a colossal ass of themselves by being someone they saw in a movie. There is not a lot of in between. I suppose it's the guys with the "in between" that can woo these women. Late into my "middle age", and seemingly aware of who I am, I'm still not sure if I'm one of these men when she is in the room. She is that kind of woman.

Nowhere near her home and seemingly far away from her life is where we first met. Strangely enough, it was over beers with another stranger. Of course, the names of who we all knew were not the issue. I knew of him, she knew of me, and isn't that where friendships start?

As "blind" meetings go, it was harmless. Johnny was the buffer. I insulted her home state in some sophomoric way. She giggled and looked sideways at me.

"So...you from Missouri?"

"Yep. Outside of St. Louis."

"Cool...what do you think of all this electricity? Isn't it somethin'?"

It's funny how love starts sometimes. You would think it would be more harps and piano playing than dumbass insults meant to draw a cheap laugh. To be honest, I couldn't think of anything else to say. She had (and still has) a presence that took me back to practically every stunning woman I ever met. That is to say, I wanted them to like me and normally what you say is supposed to be the icebreaker but it always comes out more like just plain old ice. The older I became, the more I realized that there was almost always nothing to be afraid of. More often than not, all of them were just as full of shit as I was. With Mary, she took me back to those days of intro dancing and at the same time gave me confidence to know that she wouldn't turn away, slam the door, and move on to other things. It was, without a doubt, the first time in my life I felt comfortable around strangers. Because when I think back on it...she never was.

The first part of the night worked its way out like most nights do. We talked to each other without digging too much into our pasts. We shared a few drinks. We laughed like we were old friends. And when dinner was over we caught the ferry back into town together. It was about a half hour ride from the island back to the city and dawn was setting. We sat out on the deck, shoulder to shoulder and in the span of 30 minutes we unturned the slimy rocks, unlocked the moldy trunks, and shed light on those shadows of our lives we both wanted to keep from one another. That Tuesday night on the ferry is where I truly fell for her. I've told her that so many times. I've told myself a thousand times since.

We saw each other when we could. We wrote emails and texted and called until we could plan a visit. It wasn't the perfect scenario, but it's what we had. And when the juice ran out and neither of us could bear the thought of being apart from one another...we parted. Through the empty miles and the thousands of minutes of phone calls we explored all that we could from one another without being with one another. I am guilty of holding onto her memory too closely, too tightly, too often. And when the rest of society tells me turn the page, I turn back to the deck on that boat on the water and remember her control over me.

That is the way men are supposed to feel. Now, I just wish I knew how to get rid of it.

O Me, O Life

There is an old saying that gets tossed around in church every now and then that goes something like this. "All are given the key to heaven, but that same key also opens the gates of Hell." Now, I consider myself a relatively intelligent man. I've got a few phony baloney diplomas and degrees that would prove to anyone that gives a rat's ass that certifies I'm a relatively intelligent man. And up until a few days ago, I really didn't understand what that proverb meant. I mean...I get the first part. If you treat others with respect and give a few bucks to someone that needs some food, a blanket, or a place to sleep then you'll teach your children that "charity" is not giving a hand out but a help up. By doing so, you'll probably secure for yourself a spot in your version of the afterlife. But, on the same token, if that "key" also brings about misery, pain, suffering, and an eternal death then for the love of Pete would someone explain what in the hell we would want that friggin' key for in the first place? As I mentioned, I struggled with this conflicting sentiment for years. Until recently.

Someone who I am quite fond of and know as well as you can possibly know anyone recently discovered he has cancer. It's early. It's in the beginning stages and as far as cancer goes it's not only very treatable but it's hardly a speed bump on the expressway of life. Five weeks, twice a day, and badda bing....cured. Shit, I've had hangovers that have lasted longer than that, which is what I've been trying to

43

tell this friend of mine but for some reason, he just isn't buying it. He keeps telling himself that this revelation couldn't have come at a worse time. As if there is a "good" time for this type of news. And despite the fact that the extremely small circle of friends that he has blessed with this happy little chestnut has assured him that "all will be well", he is secretly preparing his mind and heart for the emotional pitfalls before him. I've tried to tell him that while the old business adage of "expect the best but prepare for the worst" may work in the boardroom, it has no place in the mindset of something that can literally kill you from the inside out. Of course, I said it with a great deal of charm and chose to exclude buzz killer words like "kill" and "literally" but it has done very little to dissuade his perception. He feels that perhaps there is something that he has done to God and THAT is the reason that he is in this predicament. And through some seemingly valid and lucid formula in his conflicted mind, no amount of Sunday School lessons and prayers from distant friends can put off this feeling.

I asked him, repeatedly, if he is preparing to die. He assures me that is not the case. In fact, he truly feels comforted in knowing that this is - as far as cancers go - a very elementary procedure and has every chance of success. As he was discussing the procedures with me and what he is supposed to expect during this five week trip to the diet farm, he kept throwing out statistics and percentages of success rates. It seemed he was in a good place with everything that was about to happen to him. And just before I decided to pray to my God for his quick recovery, he whispered to me a chilling sentiment that is still echoing in the deepest caverns of my soul.

"Norman...I'm not ready."

With a tinge of evident destiny, he whispered what - at times - I truly believe all of us feel. Are we ever ready to make the decision in our lives to turn around when adversity confronts us or to stand up to it and thereby strengthen our own character in the process? Do we all have the fortitude to understand that sometimes life deals horribly unfair cards to us all and it is how we play them out that defines us as humans? Can you truly appreciate the moments of glory that your higher power affords you if you do not experience the rolling thunder that is pain and suffering from time to time? And lastly, who among us would not dare to use that key they are entitled to in order to explore an everlasting life of happiness all the while conveniently ignoring the faintly etched inscription on the underside of it that reads, "Just on the other side of Hell."

My point is this, my friends. I feel that subconsciously all of us are either riding the cresting waves life creates for us without troubling ourselves with the knowledge that there are sharks circling below us or we compromise our position on this earth and in the lives of others by acknowledging our frailty, embracing our mortality, and making sandwiches for our children. Which is worse? Which is better? Who in the hell cares? I told my friend that the only way to bounce back is to look up. Despite the fact that he finds himself shuffling sideways on the bottom and will continue in this existence for a while he knows that his own overall design and purpose is to not end his story this way. He recognizes that his own powerful play must continue and he still has verses to contribute to it.

What will your verse be?

Storm

During the summer of 2009 I spent a few days in the Rocky Mountains. It was mid-June, the weather forecast actually had tornado warnings in Denver, and I went up another 4,000 feet or so to Winter Park, Colorado. When I got to my cabin, it was about 75 degrees with only a few minor clouds and a slight breeze. By the time I unpacked, got on some different shoes for a hike, and went outside the wind had picked up, inky dark clouds had formed and there was that very thick smell of rain. Thunder was rolling in over the top of the peaks and lightning was flashing in every corner of the canyon. This wasn't just that distant thunder you hear and dismiss. These were the kinds of heavenly blasts of thunder you actually feel inside of your bones. I sat inside and looked out over the awesomeness of it all and just marveled on how powerful it all was and how insignificant that I felt at the time.

And then...in the matter of minutes...it was gone. And everything, after that, looked different.

I'm not sure if it was the frame of mind that I was in but that summer storm couldn't have come at a worse time. I recently have had a bit of a tempest myself in my own life. And it came on extremely suddenly, wreaked its own particular brand of havoc, and quickly rolled away. Like the squall in Winter Park, everything looks different now but at the same time there is a familiarity about it. This anomaly suggests to me that I've been here before and somehow I'll make it through again however the landscape and scenery changes. New light emerges and new sounds and scents are discovered. The lightning and wicked winds actually uncover things that you never knew were there before. People look different. They expose themselves for what they truly are and you either end up loving them even more (albeit in a completely different way) or the shell that was once created as a monument or symbol of all the things they told you have now become brittle and on the brink of shattering into a million slivers of emptiness and disappointment. You don't wish for the latter to happen and the moments that you are in this space you would give your left arm to get out of it, but...like the storm... it will pass. It's not inherent for nature to be tumultuous forever.

Nevertheless, it was destructive. I don't know where the storm is heading when it left the valley. At this point, it doesn't matter. And I would wager every penny I have left to my name that no scientific evidence could be found that a storm looks over its own shoulder to see what it has done. But I will honor and appreciate what it has left behind. It uncovered new scenery for me. It has revealed new sounds. The sound of birds and the taste of a piece of fruit and lyrics in songs all seem to possess more for me now. And if this experience has taught me anything, it's that to always keep one eye on the horizon.

I'm sure there will be more where that came from.

Critical Mass

A friend asked me the other day during a bi-monthly meeting over coffee what influences I've had in my life and who, what, when, where, (etc.) are they. We were talking about Malcolm Gladwell's book *The Tipping Point* which basically introduces a new explanation for why change happens so quickly and / or unexpectedly in people's lives, society, or within a culture. For those who are curious, "Tipping Point" – as Gladwell points out – is a phrase that epidemiologists use when an epidemic reaches critical mass.

It was a fair question and a good one. However, I was more interested in the context of the critical mass part then the influences that gets someone to that point in their life in the first place. This is a bit strange for me since I'm kind of a "root cause" type of guy, but nevertheless the storm at the moment is more interesting to me than the atmospheric conditions that brought the clouds. Why is it that way with most of us? The dangers in our lives seem to reveal the chinks in our armor, but often they open up windows into what is strong or weak or flawed or perfect in all of us. At this opening, what we see is often how we are defined. If we see perfection in the midst of chaos we are the eternal optimist looking for the light at the end of the tunnel. If we see the chaos and therefore our weakness within it then we are defined as those that just lend to the madness and a part of the overall problem of human negativity.

But then again…funks are funks. And I'm in one now. A relationship, that I very much enjoyed, recently ended and as I'm struggling to make heads or tails of whether it was my fault or whether it was the distance between us or if this departure is merely temporary until our stars align again I end up accepting the invite from this friend to have our bi-monthly examination of life over java. He hits me with his shit. I bounce mine off of him. We agree that women are – in generally – quite wicked necessities and we thank our respective gods for them on a daily basis. We promise to keep in touch. We leave.

That was the moment. That was my tipping point.

One cup of coffee is how long I stayed there and how much I was willing to invest in figuring out where my life was versus where I wanted it to go. I had really given up on thinking that I could love someone that deeply and completely. She proved me wrong. She blew in. She blew out. The energy she left behind expanded my critical mass. And I would ask all of you, my friends, to allow your life to be expanded more by letting in the bad air as well as the good. For when you do, you notice what you can accept and cannot. You see the richness of what you bring into your life more fully and you feel the mistakes that much more keenly. Your heart swells – letting more air in, letting more life in – and you become stronger and more pliable. Your breaking points become more adaptable and your heart becomes more accepting…and more forgiving.

Otherwise, the epidemic of your life will be that you just didn't allow for enough time to recognize what you need to love and what you need to leave behind.

The Leap

Rippling over the frozen grass, he sees her image arise out of the steaming ground. She is there in a long coat, head slightly tilted looking as if she is trying to remember who he is, but still smiling at him as a lover would smile upon waking after first morning light. He couldn't make himself get up any faster and didn't want to turn away for fear she would drift out of his consciousness forever...or until his next glass.

He has been driven to the precipice of his soul and forced to leap to his death and he did so gladly and without hesitation. He knew that as the blood avalanched through his body and into his brain and every emotionally charged chemical that spurns what lovers feel is electrified in his endings, he glances around him only to discover she is not there. The crags of reality are approaching at breakneck, suicidal speeds and any other man would discover the failures of his logic and recognize that leaping for her was precarious, at best.

He's unlike any other man. And she was not a risky adventure. She was the catalyst for the movement of his life toward belief in all things good and real. Whether the fall kills him or not, he'll close his eyes and feel the wind blow through his existence.

Thanksgiving

When I was little, I used to think that Thanksgiving was designed specifically for me. I feel I had every reason to believe so since my birthday fell around – and sometimes on – the actual holiday. Family got together, we had a huge feast, and at the end of it all they gave out presents and cake and sang to me. "Ooh we give to thanks to Norm… oooh oooh….. he is really, really sweet. Oooh…oooh doo wop."

Okay, so I made up the song. Sue me. But all in all, it was a pretty special time for me and my family. Not because of the birthday, of course, but the fact we got around a table – ours or others – and simply ate, laughed, and spent glorious, albeit gluttonous, moments thanking each other for our thankful thankyness. Thank you… thank you very much.

I told you that story to tell you this one. I was watching a story on ESPN some time ago about a young man in Kansas named Charlie Wilks. Charlie is a high school football player and comes from a long line of Midwestern gridiron ball players. His father played high school and college ball and his grandfather played in the NFL. He is a good sized kid with decent strength and surprising quickness for a youngster. He aspires to be a college and pro player someday, as all of us did and do who have ever strapped on a helmet and got after it under the Friday night lights.

He has some obstacles to overcome first. Charlie is blind.

And you know what Charlie is thankful for? He is thankful for his fearlessness. He is thankful for his courage. At this point in his life he is actually thankful for the sight he has been deprived of. He told ESPN, "I'm not scared of anything that's going to come to me in sports. I think my biggest fear would be getting my sight back. Once you go blind, you start imagining this world as this perfect place. Getting your sight back and seeing how imperfect it is crushes some blind people. To be honest, getting my sight back would be like another low point in my life."

As I sit among my friends this thanksgiving, I will remember Charlie. I will remember that being thankful is more than who I am, what I have or who I've become. I, of course, will be thankful for my children and the flavor they add to my life. I will be thankful for my health, which although it has failed from time to time these past few years, I'm still a functioning man in a functioning world. I will be thankful for Shelton, Portland, Mainz, Luzern, St. Louis, San Clemente, Detroit, Austin, Bellingham, Boston, Athens, Sitka, Seattle and every other place in between that has made its mark on me. And I will be thankful for my friends that have seen me through to this point and haven't gone screaming for the hills or written me off with a simple nod and dismissive glance.

But in the spirit of Charlie, I will be thankful for what I don't have. I am thankful for the world's imperfections, its flaws which make up the harmonious design of our lives. I will be thankful for those people that I have never met but have watched in the park or in the supermarket that have taught me what it means to be a good father and a good friend. I will be thankful for those people who are no longer in the mainstream of my life but who are responsible for key ingredients in my life that have developed who I am as a son, a brother, a counselor and a lover.

And I'm thankful for Charlie Wilks, a young man that possesses incredible insight and vision in the midst of a darkened world.

Oh! Christmas Tree?

There is this thought I was having a few days before Christmas last year as I went shopping for my tree. I walked through this open lot looking for the weakest, ugliest, most pathetic version of Christianity that I could find. I figured that since the symbol of the Christmas tree was initially designed to represent the immortality (Evergreens stay green all year long) and the expulsion from the Eden (apples were the original 'ornaments') then by God I was going to celebrate in all my glorious immortal sinful nature. If you can't poke fun at the fall from grace then honestly...nothing is sacred anymore. Not to mention that my children would not have appreciated hanging strings of popcorn on a fire hydrant or a large statue of Elvis.

So, the lot attendant kept asking me to consider this "...gorgeous 9 foot noble fir..." or "...have you ever had a grand fir? Oh, they're gorgeous." He was quite smitten with anything "gorgeous", as evidenced by the gorgeous wreath, gorgeous bough of holly, and gorgeous tapestry of Santa playing cards with himself that apparently made a gorgeous tree blanket that he tried to sell me. The existential ramifications of Santa playing a card game with four other members of himself notwithstanding, I found his gorgeousness to be a little creepy.

Finally, I found the perfect tree. Tucked deep behind the other $50 pretenders lay this little Douglas Fir that had – more than likely – been shoved there because it may fetch a nice asking price for those losers (like myself) that had waited to get their tree until the very last minute. I spotted it immediately and said, "That's it! That's a keeper." I could sense from Harvey the Lot Attendant (who was apparently suffering from cataracts as evidenced by the waft of medicinal herb he was emitting) that I clearly had no appreciation for Christmas tree shopping. He begrudgingly dug through the row to get to my prize, gave it a little disrespectful shake and tap on the ground, and muttered sarcastically, "She's a real beauty." I paid for my masterpiece and as Harv was strapping it onto the roof of my car I realized that I hadn't gotten a tree stand yet. I made a mental note to pick one up at Target.

Target was sold out of tree stands. Go figure. I come out into the parking lot and realize that someone had boosted my tree. I was stunned, pissed, and depressed all at once. I gazed around the parking lot looking for some Good Samaritan that may have witnessed the entire event but none were to be found.

I picked up another less meaningful but probably more visually respectable tree, made my way home, and hauled it into its proper place in the living room. Sitting down to look it over, I began thinking of how distressed someone would have to be to hijack a Christmas tree off of someone else's car. It's easy to describe these hard times as just that; hard enough to steal something that is supposed to represent goodness and mercy and peace and hope. But a Christmas tree? C'mon, people!

Then it came to me.

In a brief stroke of what I still believe to be a miraculous whisper from God, I recognized that this minor theft is nothing more than a symbol of what some people cannot give to their families. It may have been a desperate attempt made by one father that feels his life to be slipping away from him. He may feel that the only thing he can do to reinforce some normalcy in his life and in the lives of his children is to have a tree in the corner adorned with one string of lights and paper snowflakes made by his 1st grader. What may have seemed like a despondent petty theft may have actually been a young mother's attempt at securing peace in her heart despite the years of abuse from every man in her life. Perhaps it was even a teenager's desperate plea for a return to a Christmas he once knew as a child because the only one he'd ever known since then were spent under bridges, in lines at a shelter, or in an emergency room.

I felt a little ashamed at my holiday funk and decided that this tree would be perfect. I thought of my children and my family and how much I've been given and how fortunate I am. I thought of a good friend's comments to me recently about how sometimes the only gift that some men and women can give to their children is not genetically passing along their addiction to heroin. I thought of my friends and how I would truly be lost without their love, support, and patience in this ever developing – but well meaning – train wreck that is Norman Gilbert. And I thought of God...and how much He has truly saved a wretch like me.

O Christmas tree, o' Christmas tree...how lovely are your branches.

Just Above Rock Bottom

I think Ebeneezer Scrooge was on to something. Granted, he wasn't the most gracious of men and he probably wasn't asked to partake in the office fantasy football league or invited to happy hour with the accounting team, but all in all I think he wasn't half bad. I know what you're thinking. "Rawlings is going somewhere with this and going to try to flip it into some meaningful pile of steaming goo that is supposed to make me feel good or try to turn my attention toward the Christmas spirit." Let me first say that if you are thinking that then you need to get out more because if you ARE thinking that, and you need me to point you in the direction of Christmas spirit then brother.. no amount of my drivel will get that fire going for you and I am the LAST person you need to turn to in order to find meaning in this holiday season.

But then again, that is my point, I guess. Scrooge was who he was. His life was spent on manipulating the system. He used every tool in his arsenal to douse cold water on any emotional investment people tried to create in the workplace as he felt it was counterproductive to the bottom line. All he was guilty of was not subscribing to the theory that happy employees make better employees. Frankly, I wouldn't mind if old Scrooge was running our Federal Reserve. Take emotion out of the picture. Keep banks running. Keep businesses open. Keep people employed. I just wouldn't have him as my Human Resources Director or Chief Morale Officer. Nevertheless, he's tagged as some sort of fiscal tightwad, sentimental miser and crotchety old bastard. Poor, poor Ebeneezer.

But was he really all that bad? What did he really do that was all that appalling? We condemn him as the miser of Christmas simply because he worked himself into a position in his life where he was forced to see things that weren't there. He spent so much of his time keeping his people on the production line rather than on the unemployment line that he slowly started to creep toward rock bottom himself and as we all know, Rock Bottom is that wonderful, enchanting Mecca where fun and wonderfulness happens. Scrooge showed us the way to that place. He blazed the path toward Rock Bottom, hovered above it tempestuously for what seemed like years, watched his friend and business partner die, and crept ever so slowly and more closer toward death. We label him as the mayor of Grinchville when all he did was struggle to overcome what was – I'm sure –a faltering economy in his day. Who among us hasn't felt the sting of similar fates? And what did he receive in return? Insanity. His efforts were the catalyst for mental imaginings from ungrateful spooks who clearly couldn't see his vision of a more financially secure existence among the other pirates of Wall Street. Dickens pigeonholed Scrooge and painted him as the poster boy for Bad Gone Good. DAMN YOU, DICKKKKKENNNNNS!!!

Who hasn't been there? Who hasn't hit Rock Bottom, hit it and started to dig, or have a time share on Rock Bottom Boulevard. Sometimes in our mixed up days and sleepless nights, we are gradually cornering ourselves or drifting along with the currents toward a place where the only enlightenment we'll ever find is thrusted upon us by non-earthly motivating factors such as fate, love, or misery. I've been there myself. And before I break into my best baritone and sing "Nobody knows the trouble I've seen. Nobody knows my sorrow", stand by this thought for a second. Scrooge paved the way for all of us. We may not go around humbugging anything that reeks of goodness and decency, but I would bet my daughter's last bag of sour gummy worms that we don't go looking for these moments and people in our life either and try to impart the positive in our life to them. If you're doing that then good on you. Let me know how that goes, however I would imagine that most of us are waiting for the ghosts to come in some form or fashion. And I'll be damned if these ghouls are lining up at our door to come to us in the middle of the night with the clear picture of what we are supposed to do with the rest of our lives. I don't know how your ghosts show up, but mine typically don't have words of wisdom for my weary soul. My god...I'd welcome any poltergeist into my bed chamber if they could illuminate a clear path toward enlightenment and happiness. You hear that Casper? Come on over. My door is unlocked. In the meantime, my argument would be that the world needs a Scrooge or two to either show us the way to Rock Bottom so we can avoid that route or as an example of how to rebound with a clear conscious and a warmer approach to life.

Finally, if you want a real rock bottom, feel good movie of the year then I have one for you. This guy and his wife are riding into town flat broke. She's pregnant to the point of delivery at a moment's notice, he's an out of work carpenter, and they are bumping along straddling their only asset. No room at the hotel. No friends or family's couch to crash on. It's the dead of night and she's ready to burst. They find a barn, it's cold and dark, and they are starving. Sounds like rock bottom to me. As I recall, things turned out ok for them...and for the rest of us.

So cut old Scrooge some slack folks. He was a trend setter and ahead of his time. After all, you never know what kind of miracle you'll find just above rock bottom. We have Ebeneezer to thank for that.

My Resolution

I'm going to let you all in on a little background secret of mine. Before I toiled in the phone business or became an aspiring writer and before I sold Long Distance plans door to door, and even before I sold beer and wine… I was a funeral director. I'll allow a timely pause while everyone gives their collective "ewwww" and in the meantime point out that it was a very logical and mature decision of moving into that line of work and not one spurned on by morbid curiosity or some sick sense of the macabre. Despite the drunken tours of the funeral home that I gave to visiting friends, ("dude….got any dead bodies in the house?") for the most part I took my job very seriously. Oh sure…there were moments of unnerving hilarity. For instance, I dare you to stop laughing during an Irish wake for Grandpa Patty when a drunken brawl breaks out… at the graveside…. on Easter Sunday… involving the widow…and the priest. Not many know of the rituals involving graveside services and even fewer may be cognizant of the traditions of a good Irish wake, but I'll bet you the last beer in my fridge that they don't involve lifting the priest and an old woman out of a six foot hole.

So, the job had its relatively sensible "high points", but as you can imagine any profession whose many individual purposes include escorting our fellow human sufferers away from their grief and toward healing (and a profit) there was more gray and black than rose and cheery. The list which illustrates this is too long and regrettably too engrained in my memory to recount. And since that is not my overall point it's best to leave my recollection still giggling over old Uncle Mick struggling drunkenly to help his mother out of the hole, Grandma Patty spitting curses toward all of the "bastard leaches after her plot", and Father Harold wondering if $250 was worth getting punched in the mouth from the bony hand of a 90 year old leprechaun.

Death has a way of being funny to some. Hollywood has assured us of this. It has a way of ruining a perfectly good day for others. And still for some of us, we struggle with understanding what it will do, why it has to happen, and what to become of it when the dust to dust settles. I rarely torture myself with such thoughts considering I've seen death relatively first hand. I say "relatively" as up until this past holiday season, I've always been a spectator in what is otherwise someone else's grief. Even some friends, a few family members, and work acquaintances untimely passing have gone skipping over the top of my emotional and intellectual surface like a flat rock across glassy water.

That all changed on the day before Christmas Eve, 2009.

From a top floor of a downtown Portland parking garage, a 15 year old boy leapt to his death directly in front of me. What is even more chilling is that his mother was even closer than I was and the last thing she saw was her son's feet go over the edge of the cement wall. I rushed to the side only to see him crashing to the street below and the only sound I heard after that (and seemingly every night since) was his mother's uncontrollable scream. It was a sound I'll never forget. It was a simultaneous howl to God and Satan in such pitches and at such a volume that there was no mistaking it for anything other than primordial and insane.

The rest of the episode will be spared because, quite frankly, no one ever needs to hear it or even imagine it again. I only bring it up to galvanize my state of being in the coming new year. Recently, I reached out to all of my friends on Facebook to tell them to take their children aside and tell them you love them; an innocuous task, to be sure, but often one that gets lost in all of our other day to day meanderings. And even more often than the simple and quick "Love ya" to our kids is the numbing state of affairs our daily lives bring and how it sometimes cheapens what we are doing for our children and – more intensely – what they are doing for us. Through the media, I discovered some of the facts that surrounded this young boy's death and the darkness that had descended on their family. I can't help but wondering if this darkness came completely unbeknownst to the boy's mother. The bridge that parents attempt to gap between the hardships of our day to day lives and the lives of our children (whom we mistakenly think are stress and care free) is getting harder and harder to construct. Technology, the arts, attention spans, outside influences, etc. are so incredibly overwhelming to all of us that they are driving a wedge between the simplest connection of father and son, mother and daughter. It has to start with those simple words and simple actions of "I love you" and then embracing your children before they feel that the only option is the last option. Make them see the bridge…not the way off of it.

I'll convene these disturbing images with this final thought: There is not one member of my family nor any of my close friends that I would not want to stand next to and offer encouragement and some measure of comfort to if it only meant you found some hope in this world and imparted that hope and happiness to those in your circles, and those in their circles, and so on. I challenge any of you reading to give yourself the time to understand the time of others. By doing so, you will be able to capture what Winston Churchill meant when he said, "You make a living by what you get. You make a life by what you give."

That is my New Year's resolution. **That** is the only one I'll ever make.

One Step

It was only a blackened road glistening from the new rain and the breaking moonlight but standing in the wet grass only one step off of the cement he felt it was like a perilous abyss that would devour him if he dared to cross it. The flickering streetlight showed slight depressions and the faded white lines but it still didn't convince him. He knew that the second he stepped onto the street there was no turning back.

She was only a train ride away. A few short hours north and she would be there at the taxi stand waiting for him. Without really knowing why, he'd walk up to her and take her in his arms and press her head on his chest. She'll breathe him into her lost heart. He'll close his eyes and let her hair touch his lips and feel his arms strengthen around her sobbing shoulders. The aching of their emptiness could melt away despite the dense chill of the October air.

The hour will be late when he arrives. There will be very few people on the train going that far north that late into the evening. He would be thankful for that. He almost looked forward to the darkened passenger car and the shadows of the countryside clicking by. His pack had the necessities; a change of clothes, six beers, and a picture. The beers were easily accessible. The picture was years away.

He wanted to step forward. He wanted to run to her. He begged his body to move and not look back over his shoulder to where he could see the front porch light of his home across the park. He cursed at himself for thinking about what he'd say to her and how he would explain the hopelessness he was bringing to her doorstep. He had nothing left to give her. Any semblance of the man she knew was abandoned months after he slipped away under hushed tones and a whisper in her sleeping ear. He found what he was always afraid to find and in those years since he left had been trying to make his way back to her. He cursed again as he looked down on his wet boots and the bottomless step off the curb. He reached into his pack, pulled out a beer and in a deft move opened it as he brought it to his lips.

He turned away from the street, away from the station, and away from her....back into the darkness of his life.

Help Me Understand This

Sometimes, there are so many things that just completely elude my comprehension. I'm not talking about molecular physics or neuro-technology. I'm talking about the things that comprise our day to day world that men of my age...anyone of my age...should probably know at this point in their life. My brain is crammed with useless facts and random quotes from a thousand different sources and some feeble network to be able to make them relevant to whatever the hell I'm talking about at the time, but for the most part I don't know how to make things make sense. For instance, I'm not entirely sure why people say steak is supposed to be bad for you. The people that don't like ice cream scare the shit out of me. I can't put together two coherent thoughts regarding Californians, even though I love most all of them that I have met and I was actually born there. I don't get why my son has such amazing, intrinsically woven traits like his great grandfather's eyes and his mother's intelligence...but he can't, for the life of him, flush the damn toilet after he pees. No one can convince me that long distance relationships are doomed to fail from the start. And for the love of God would someone please explain to me Miley Cyrus? Because I'm just not getting it.

These are but a few that rattle around in my brain and stir up just enough dust to coat my intellect with a nice film of stupidity. As it is with dust in my home, it generally doesn't bother me too much until I happen upon it or until the sun shines through and reveals its presence and then you are forced to deal with it. Often times, however, when the dust settles it reveals other things that are far more serious and require me to take notice to them. For instance, why is there so much power in this world to create energy and heat but people still freeze to death in their homes? If we can chemically alter plants to make mind altering drugs, why can't we put a couple of herbs together to make sure babies never die? And what makes a man so void of hope and peace in his life that he deems it a viable solution to put a gun in his mouth rather than pick up the phone and ask for help?

Sometimes, I get so damn mad I can't sleep anymore. I'm awake at all hours wondering about the sense of it all. And the more I think about it the more dust that seems to drift up into my consciousness powdering even more of my idiocy. I suppose it's a natural course of events that we are not to know all of the answers to everything. It seems like life would be pretty damn boring if we had every solution to every problem. Kind of like doing a children's crossword puzzle, I suppose. But for the love of friggin' Pete, there are some things that we *have* to know that we currently don't. Thank God there are smarter people than I.

I suppose all I need is sunshine – in all its forms and through all of its carriers – to flash light on the dust of my world so I will continue to ask myself these questions in hopes that I discover some element of truth amongst the madness. Because when it comes right down to it, folks...if we can't figure this stuff out, what the hell are we doing here?

Tuesday Night

It's a rough life, sometimes, living in the Pacific Northwest and not being able to look upon the Seattle skyline and the water and the ferries crossing the Sound and not think of that Tuesday night. For the life of him, he can't remember any other night in his life quite as clearly as that one. Surely, if he had known that the earth would come to a halt and the air would leave all corners of the city when he saw her then he would have put on a better pair of pants. As it turned out, he had no answer to the deafening silence when she entered the room. He had no lines to give her, as was his typical pitch on these types of occasions. As ridiculous as it sounds, he thought of grass and sand and that very first breath of wind in the spring that convinces you that you've seen the end of a long, cold winter. Her eyes was a spectrum for every flicker of light in the room and when she laughed it was like hearing love and friendship speak to you personally.

They shared the ferry ride with a friend out to the island. They shared it alone coming back into the city. They shared a bottle of champagne served by Gay Troy and his merry band of busboy stalkers. They shared the ride back to the hotel. They shared the night together. And in doing so they touched a life within each other that had only been imagined but dismissed. They learned who they truly were supposed to be rather than what they had become. They learned that all of the anger, bitterness, humiliation and hopelessness that ravage our souls can be washed away with laughter, silent caresses, and trust. What was wrong and broken in their lives evaporated into the darkness of a foggy Seattle midnight.

He didn't want to leave. He still doesn't want to leave. In the years that have passed and the years yet to come, he'll draw from the memory of that night and in so doing be able to sand out the jagged edges of his life. He'll remember that there, beside the Seattle piers, his own version of purity was validated. He will know that it does exist and not just "once upon a time" or "fade to black." When needed, he will gather that memory and hold it near to his face so he can feel its warmth and smell the ocean breeze again.

Tuesday nights in Seattle will last forever.

My Waffle Dream

For the last 30 years, I've been having this strange semi-recurring dream. It borders on the classification of nightmarish and disturbing and just when I've got the phone in hand to call Wes Craven on a movie deal it will show up again but only this time it has a spin toward the light hearted where everyone eats waffles and sings and ultimately doesn't die in the end. Regardless of the ending, I wake up shaking, gasping for breath, or craving bananas and maple syrup. I like bananas on my waffles.

The air is heavy and cold in this dream. I'm walking down a heavily overgrown and long abandoned logging road behind my uncle's house outside of Shelton, Washington. What light that is left of the dying day is being choked away by the darkening night. The silence is absolutely overpowering. I hear nothing but my own pounding heart and the deep echoes of my panting breath through my lungs. My head slowly swivels from one side of the path to the next half expecting to be swallowed violently by the undergrowth. The shadows of the forest are etched in mist and cut off from the ground as if they are hovering in limbo waiting to be a part of the earth. It's an eerie existence for them. It's a terrifying one for me.

I'm looking for something....or someone. I have this hidden awareness somewhere in my being that time is running out. There is no ticking clock. The only semblance of passing time exists in the darkening sky, although that exudes a more foreboding sensation than the elapse of seconds and minutes. The later versions of my dream have my thoughts turning to my children. Some nights they are the key to my urgency in getting down this road and sometimes I have a keen understanding that they are far from this place and safely tucked away in their own beds wrapped snugly within innocent dreams of Nerf guns, baby jaguars, and red vine licorice. Some nights long gone friends from my childhood will make cameo appearances. They never really show up in person, but their presence is made clear in the framework of the shadows. It feels as if they are in danger or their lives are coming to an end and I've only got a few brief moments to find them, save them, or lose them to eternity.

My brother and sister are there with me on selected occasions. Again, I am alone on this path but their spirit flows through me and I'm either reminded of younger, happier days where we barbecued, ate homemade waffles, and played Monopoly at the top of the stairs until one of us was bankrupt and pissed off at the nature of our own make believe economy. They play bit parts in this dream, which is apropos since they've played relatively minor (yet incredibly starring) roles in my life as an adult.

And then one night, a few years back, the road emptied onto a field. The darkness became dusk again and the light of the sun gave birth to brilliant colors of such a dancing warmth that I knew that there, in the darkness of my room wrapped in my own covers, I cried tears of pure joy. The road ended at a field and across the field was a slow flowing river. It was there that I met an angel. It was there that I met the mate of my soul. As Caliban from Shakespeare's *The Tempest* said: "...that when I awoke I cried to dream again." That version has never come appeared before...or since.

To approach the dream on a less somber note, it does provide me a glorious opportunity to rediscover old friends and happy memories. I recall waking up and for the next few days, weeks or months blissfully recalling back yard ball games which resulted in childhood heroes. I sit preoccupied with the soft and sweet memory of fresh cut grass and morning first pitches of little league games when they actually meant something. I recall the intensity of board games and flying pieces and cash changing hands in exchange for properties or the last bite of pizza. I remember the 800 pound waffle maker and the batter dripping down its side and my job of cutting up the exact number of banana slices that would fit onto each piece. I remember first kisses and shy moments. I remember the bound in faith contract of a simple note being passed in history class which read, "Will you go with me?" resulting in a cataclysmic display of bravery of walking down the hallway hand in hand for all the world to see.

The dreams brought to the surface the innocent bystanders, participants, and loves of my life. They resurrected the passions of those that stood shoulder to shoulder with me on the hilarity of being a boy and the perils of becoming a man. They were there for it all: Movie quotes, rounds of golf, long hikes toward the heavens, days of drinking, nights of lovemaking, agonizing side splitting fits of uncontrollable laughter, and road trips to nowhere for the purposes of nothing were all born by the accomplices within this emission of my mind. I would wake to consider these people and their memories and longingly ponder the development they've had in my life.

Now…I suppose that the psychological interpretations of the versions of this recurring dream are bountiful. Freud and the rest of his coke whore buddies would go bonkers with suggestions that the dark forest represents my dark and unexplored psyche or conversely that the density of the trees might foretell of the richness of my life yet the unexplored caverns of happiness unseen and a joy yet discovered. I, for one, think that the majority of dream interpretation is either 90 percent bullshit and 10 percent reality leakage or 10 percent stress and 90 percent God. Either way, it's up to the dreamer and not Sigmund to answer those questions.

Despite the outcomes of the dream or the participants or the manner in which I awake it always leads me to the same conclusion. I am lost and searching or I have found my Eden and it is incomplete. I prefer the latter as it suggests that our heaven is what we make of it. It is the heaven of friends and family. It is the events of our lives and the memories born of it and the freedom to create our own "happily ever after" that are the boundaries of our eternal bliss. They are the "streets of gold" that await us all. I believe that is what God has created for me and has meant for the time after I am long gone from this earth. And even if you don't buy into this line of thinking certainly you can recognize that there exists something better and bigger outside of our waking hours. Whether this existence resides in the ongoing lives of your children or those that you love, or if it is encompassed in the continuing development of the world around you, is something only you can decide.

And lastly, whether you believe in God or not...I do wish for the realization of your continuance of mind, body, and spirit. If, for no other reason, that none of us deserve to be forgotten on a dead quiet, dark and forgotten path, cold and alone. I suppose that this "continuance" is the stuff dreams are made of.

For me...I hope they have waffles.

Parting Shots...

On this rainy November morning in the great Pacific Northwest, I find myself on the doorstep of a new beginning. For the last 7 months, I've been living out of suitcases, cars, homeless shelters, and even an abandoned garage for a night. There have been couches, air mattresses, broken futons, and borrowed beds. Dinner has come from a bag, a microwave, and from kitchens of angels, both men and women alike. My body has changed. My mind has reshifted. My heart has softened. Those that love me have stayed; those that did have resurfaced. I can't help but wonder if it is all some sort of master plan to move me from the depths and deathly stillness of the middle of the ocean toward some current that will sweep me in the direction of paradise.

The Roman philosopher, Seneca, wrote "Most men ebb and flow in wretchedness between the fear of death and the hardship of life; they are unwilling to live and yet they do not know how to die." As I write this, I'm coming to the crystal realization that over the last 12 months I've visited the cavern of life's hardships and have seen death distantly from the front entrance overlooking my existence. It has been through the love of others that I have made it through the storm. They have comforted me, fed me, given me peace and clarity to my thoughts and literally – at times – lifted me to my feet and washed the dirt from my body. I grew up learning that pulling yourself up by the bootstraps is the first step in recovery. I'll do you one better. Opening your eyes to your surroundings and focusing in on the hearts around you that were once blurred by your own selfish, distorted visions is the first step to gaining your stability in this world. I'll take brothers over bootstraps any day of the week.

As I'm writing this, my weekend with my kids is approaching. I'll make the two hour drive to see them and consequently the two hour drive back to where I'm staying. We've played every road game known to mankind. We've sang every song we know, stopped by every roadhouse diner, and pulled over to play catch or find crickets at every rest stop along the way. It's a ritual that has been in existence for us since they were young "babies". I don't mind it so much anymore. It is good time with them. We giggle hysterically; plays made up games, and have even prayed to God at 70 miles per hour.

My children know that despite any hardships that I've gone through that they will always be able to see clearly my love for who they are, their presence in my life, and who they have made me become. Isn't it great that children can have such clarity of vision while the rest of us wear bi-focals? What is it that distorts our perspective so much that we fail to see the purity of life and love that floods us on a daily basis? How can we allow all those that love us to clear away our path and make it more unobstructed? I suppose for some of us, myself included, that is the real secret to life. That is…how to get the hell out of our own way and let love take over.

For me…from now on…I will look close to me first to see the truth and the answers to my life. Then, I will gaze out over the distance to re-discover those nights, those laughs, and those memories that have made me and realize that they weren't as blurry as I made them out to be. I've only come to this realization in the past few weeks. I hope it's not too late.

Who knows? Maybe along my line of sight I'll discover all of you looking back out of your caves at me. If I do…I'll wave and smile… whether I know you or not.

LaVergne, TN USA
11 March 2011
219870LV00001B/180/P